# NEGOTIATIONS

Anne Laws

**Summertown**
Publishing

Negotiations

Published by
Summertown Publishing Ltd,
32-38 Saffron Hill
London
EC1N 8FH

Summertown Publishing is an imprint of Marshall Cavendish Ltd. a member of the Times
Publishing Group

ISBN 978-1-902741-24-6

First published 2000
Reprinted 2004, 2005, 2006, 2008, 2009 (twice)

Produced for Summertown Publishing by the
Linguarama Group Pedagogical Unit.

Printed by Zrinski d.d., Croatia

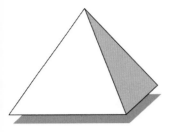

# Contents

## Part One: Phases

## Part Two: Approach

# Part Three: Evaluation

# Use of symbols in this book

This warning symbol indicates **common problems** and **important points**.

This refers to other chapters or sections with relevant information.

This indicates **useful advice** to help you achieve a successful outcome.

This symbol is used to indicate a '**hint**' or **suggestion** to improve your negotiating skills.

This symbol indicates important **cultural points**.

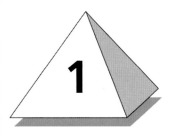

# Introduction to this book

Negotiation is often regarded as something rather complicated and specialised. People tend to forget that, in many areas of business, negotiation takes place even though it may not be on a formal basis. In fact, we all negotiate regularly in our daily life with members of our family and with friends and colleagues at work.

## What is negotiation?

Negotiating involves two or more individuals or groups of people communicating with each other, hoping to reach agreement about something.

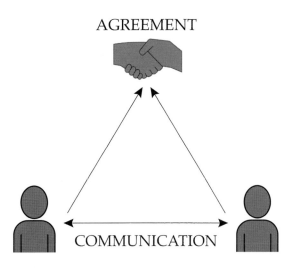

# About this book

This book is divided into three parts.

- **Part One: Phases**
  The stages a negotiation goes through and the language used at each stage.

- **Part Two: Approach**
  Your approach to negotiation: cultural differences and other problems.

- **Part Three: Evaluation**
  Assessing how the negotiation went.

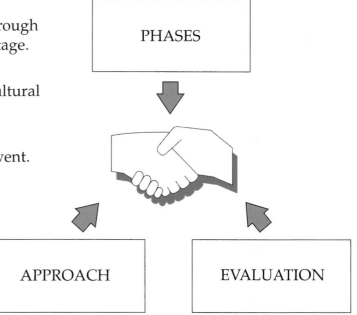

# Part One: Phases

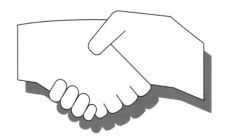

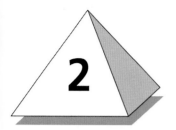

# **Phases of negotiation**

In order to reach agreement, all negotiations go through the following phases:

- Preparation
- Establishing rapport
- Discussion: starting the negotiation
- Proposals
- Bargaining
- Reaching settlement

In each phase, you will apply different skills and use different aspects of language. This book describes these phases of negotiation, the skills and the English that you will need for each phase.

## Negotiating language

Language is a very important aspect of negotiation and many business people of all nationalities have to negotiate in English. It is useful to think about the language that you will need for each phase of a negotiation.

Some examples are shown on the next page.

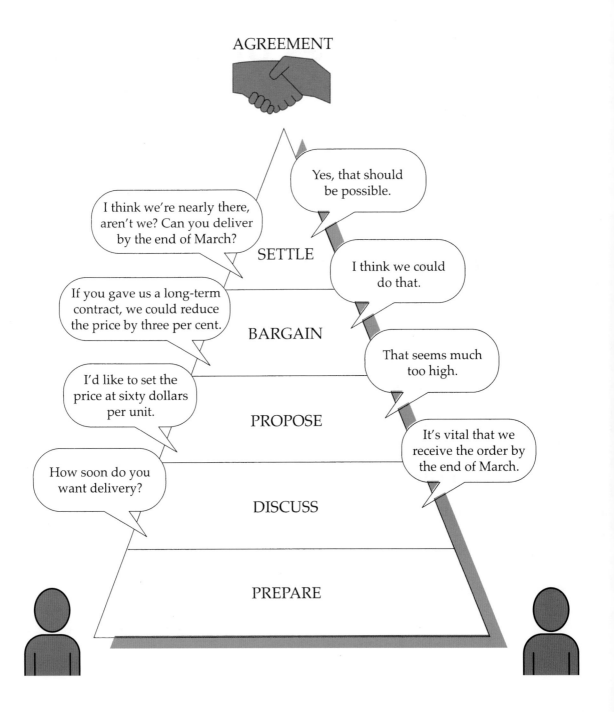

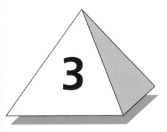

# Preparation

**3**

Preparation is the first stage of the negotiation process.

- A lack of preparation can result in failure to reach a satisfactory agreement.
- A negotiator who is well prepared will be more successful than one who is not so well prepared. It is not easy to 'think on your feet'. Preparation will help you to organise your thoughts before you start to negotiate.

PREPARE

## How should you prepare?

Start by considering

- the issues involved
- your interests
- your objectives
- the other party's interests.

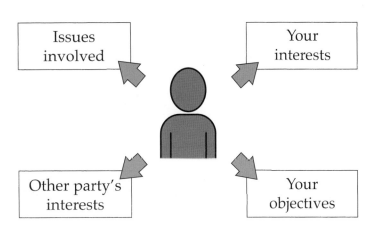

Issues involved

Your interests

Other party's interests

Your objectives

# Identify what the issues or problems are

The purpose of negotiating is to discuss an issue or a problem with another party in the hope or expectation of reaching an agreement.

In many negotiations, there are several issues or problems. Make sure that you know what they are.

## Examples

| SUBJECT OF THE NEGOTIATION | ISSUES OR PROBLEMS THAT COULD EXIST |
|---|---|
| You are trying to sell a product to a customer | • The customer might not want to buy it.<br>• The customer might agree to buy it but will argue about the price, the product's quality or the delivery date.<br>• You must make a profit from selling the product. |
| You are negotiating with representatives of your work force about pay and working conditions | • The work force want more pay and better working conditions.<br>• You do not have enough money to give them what they want. Your company must reach its financial targets. |
| You are negotiating with representatives of other countries about fishing quotas | • There is a danger that the number of fish in the sea will become too low.<br>• Each country wishes to protect its fishermen and fishing industry. |

# Identify your interests

In any negotiation about an issue or a problem, each party has certain interests that it wants to defend or promote.

An interest is not a specific objective or target. It is something that is a matter of fundamental concern. You should not reach any agreement in a negotiation that damages your interests or puts your interests at risk.

## Examples

| SUBJECT OF THE NEGOTIATION | INTERESTS THAT COULD EXIST |
|---|---|
| In a negotiation to sell a product | <ul><li>The profits of your company.</li><li>Getting a good price from selling the product.</li><li>In the longer term, having a good relationship with the customer.</li></ul> |
| In a negotiation to buy a product | <ul><li>Getting 'value' for the money you spend.</li><li>In the longer term, having a good relationship with the supplier.</li></ul> |
| In a political negotiation | <ul><li>The safety of your citizens.</li><li>The prosperity of your citizens.</li><li>The economic interests of your country.</li></ul> |

The interests of each party will be different. This is why they must meet to negotiate an agreement. The aim of a negotiation should be to **reconcile the interests** of both parties.

In many negotiations, both parties have some interests in common ('common ground'). When you look for common interests with the other party, you will have a good chance of reaching an agreement in the negotiation.

## Example: common interests

When representatives of the management of a company meet representatives of the staff to negotiate pay and working conditions, each party will share some common interests.

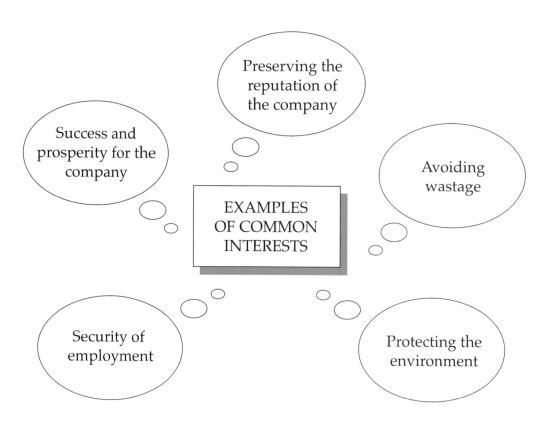

# Interests and positions

It is important to understand the difference between '**interests**' and '**positions**'.

|  | EXAMPLE: A NEGOTIATOR FOR THE EMPLOYEES OF A COMPANY |
|---|---|
| **INTERESTS**<br><br>'**Interests**' are matters of fundamental concern. Close examination of interests may reveal common ground with the other party. | • Good pay for the employees.<br>• Good working conditions for the employees.<br>• Security of employment. |
| **POSITION**<br><br>A '**position**' is an attitude that you adopt after consideration of your interests. | • Insist on an increase in pay of 3%.<br>• Insist on a reduction in working hours to 34 hours each week.<br>• Refuse to agree to the employer's demand to reduce the size of the work force by 5%. |

Skilled negotiators concentrate on interests rather than positions.

Positional bargaining emphasizes conflict, not common ground.

You might change your **position** at any time during a negotiation but your **interests** should not change.

## Set your bargaining objectives

When you have identified and prioritised your interests, you should think about the specific objectives you want to achieve from the negotiation.

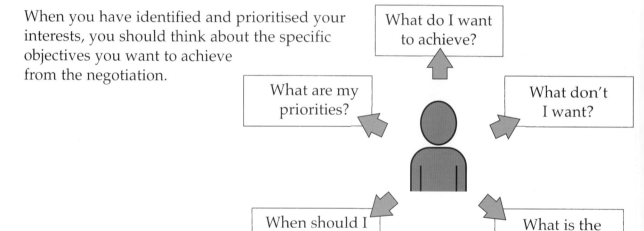

What do I want to achieve?

What are my priorities?

What don't I want?

When should I stop negotiating?

What is the most I can lose?

### What do you want to achieve?

In most negotiations, you should have a **range of objectives**, not only one. For example, you may wish to buy some goods but that is not the only objective. You probably want to buy them at the most reasonable price and you also want to receive the goods as quickly as possible.

Remember: The more objectives you focus on, the more room you have for bargaining.

## What are your priorities?

You should **prioritise** your objectives. ('Prioritise' means put them in order of importance.) For example, you can consider what is your **ideal result** or the best result that you can get, **what you can expect to get** and **what is just acceptable** (although you hope to achieve more than this).

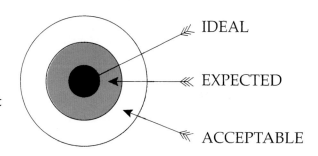

Here is another way of listing your priorities:

| WHAT I MUST ACHIEVE | WHAT I HOPE TO ACHIEVE | OTHER POSSIBLE ACHIEVEMENTS |
|---|---|---|
|  |  |  |

Your first attempt to list your objectives might not be perfect. You will probably change your objectives and your priorities when you think about other things.

## What don't you want?

When you list your objectives, think about **what you don't want to agree to**, as well as what you do want to achieve.

## When should you stop negotiating?

When you list your objectives you should think carefully about the minimum that you must achieve from the negotiation. You can do this by thinking about the consequences of not reaching an agreement. If you cannot reach an agreement with the other party, what will happen?

In the US and Britain, some negotiators call this the '**Best Alternative to Negotiated Agreement**' or '**BATNA**'. This term was first devised by the Harvard Negotiation Project in 'Getting to Yes', Fisher and Ury, Arrow Business Books.

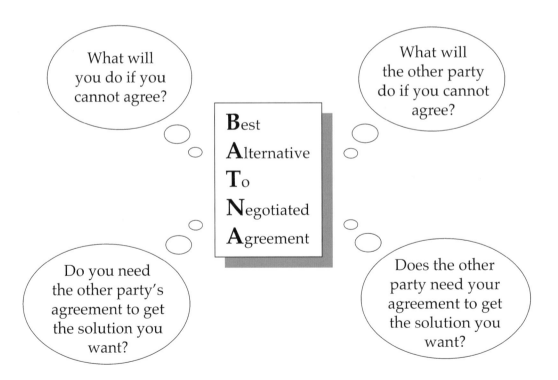

You should not reach an agreement that puts you in a worse position than the BATNA. The objectives that you set as your 'acceptable' target should be better than the BATNA.

## What is the most you can lose?

Another way of thinking about your minimum objectives is to ask yourself: '**What is the most I can lose if I agree to what the other party wants?**'.

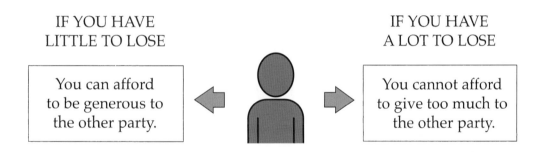

IF YOU HAVE
LITTLE TO LOSE

You can afford
to be generous to
the other party.

IF YOU HAVE
A LOT TO LOSE

You cannot afford
to give too much to
the other party.

## Research the other party

You should try to learn as much as possible about the other party.

- Who will you be negotiating with?
- What type of people are they?
- What will the other party want to achieve from the negotiation?

## Who will you be negotiating with?

Find out as much as possible about:

- their company
- their department
- their cultural background
- their country.

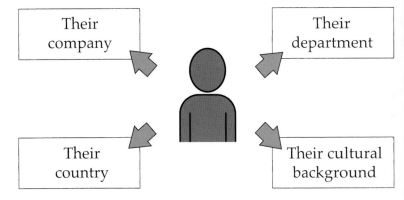

You can do this by reading their company literature and by talking to your colleagues who may have negotiated with them before.

If possible, find out something about the personal characteristics of the individuals in their negotiating team.

## Exchange useful information

It might be a good idea to exchange information with the other party before you meet.

For example, you might be meeting with the other party to negotiate the details of a document, such as a legal contract.

You could send a copy of the document (a 'draft' copy) to the other party to read before the meeting. This will save a lot of time when you meet because the other party will be better prepared.

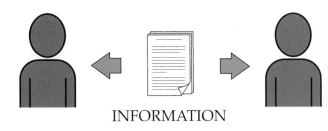

INFORMATION

## Assess the other party's interests

Think about what the other party will want to achieve from the negotiation. You should try to 'put yourself in their shoes'.

If you were in their position,

- what would be their interests and
- what would you be trying to achieve?

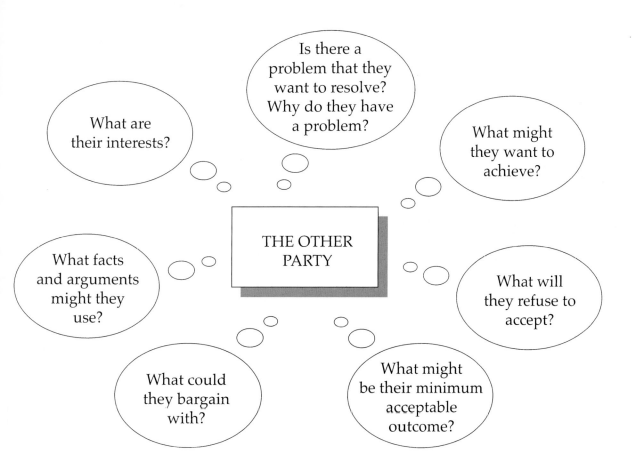

# Common ground

When you and the other party do not have an immediate or obvious answer to the problem, it is important to consider the likely common ground (common interests) between you and the other party.

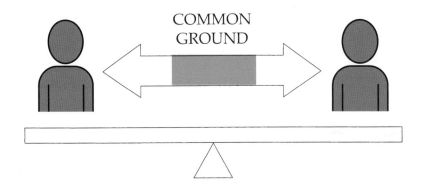

This will create a positive negotiating climate and so will help to achieve agreement. This is particularly advisable when the negotiation is part of a long-term relationship.

For example, in a negotiation about a reduction in the number of employees:

| INTERESTS OF EMPLOYER | COMMON GROUND | INTERESTS OF WORK FORCE |
|---|---|---|
| Reduce costs and improve profitability by reducing work force. | Prevent company from closure and therefore protect **most** jobs. | Protect workers' interests. No enforced redundancies. |

When preparing, you can use the following forms to make notes about the other party.

## Individual characteristics

Individual's name

Organisation / department

Position

Nationality

Experience

Now consider the other party's interests and objectives.

## Other party's interests and objectives

Their interests

Their main objectives

Other likely objectives

Their likely minimum objectives

What could they bargain with?

Now consider any likely reactions the other party may have to your proposals:

## Their likely reactions to my proposals

Anticipated objections

My reply to their objections

Common ground

Possible compromises

At this stage in your preparation, you might decide to alter your own objectives.

# Preparing to bargain

You should also think about how you might bargain with the other party.

Calculate the value of what you can trade with the other party - both the value to you and the value to them. It is important not just to give things away. There may be things which are of little value to you but which are valuable to them. Add up the value of everything you are prepared to trade. If the cost is too high for you, you will not achieve your ideal objective so you should reconsider the package you are offering.

List all the issues on which you are willing to trade.

| WHAT COULD BE OFFERED | WHAT I COULD ASK FOR IN RETURN |
| --- | --- |
|  |  |

# Strengths and weaknesses

In a negotiation, each party may have some strengths and weaknesses. It is important to recognise what these are.

| IF YOU HAVE... | LIKELY OUTCOME |
|---|---|
| A strength | You can expect to achieve more from the negotiation. |
| A weakness | You will probably have to make a fairly big concession to the other party. |
| Strengths and weaknesses | You should be willing to compromise to reach an agreement. |

There are different kinds of strengths and weaknesses.

- superior knowledge of the subject of the dispute
- superior financial resources
- the greater moral strength of your case
- authority: you are the boss, negotiating with subordinates
- time is on your side. You do not need a quick resolution to the problem whereas the other party does
- better preparation.

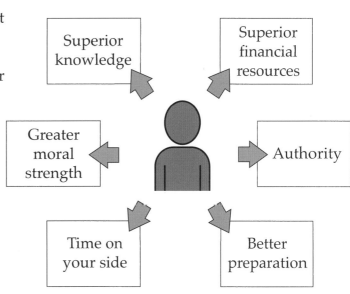

Remember that your perception of your own strengths and weaknesses may not be the same as the other party's perception of them.

## Prepare a statement of interests

At the beginning of the negotiation, you and the other party will outline your interests. It is useful, especially if you are using a foreign language, to prepare your statement of interests before the negotiation. You need to feel confident about what you are going to say.

The initial statement of interests is important because people will make judgements about you. You need to look and sound confident.

You may prefer to **make notes on cards** so that you do not have to read out your statement from a sheet of paper.

The notes will remind you of all the important points you need to mention.

## Example: a statement of interests

Your company wishes to buy a new computer system for its marketing department. It is your job to negotiate the purchase. You are meeting the representative of a software company.

1. My company's marketing department has been using the same computer system for seven years and now wants a new one.

2. We want the new system soon but we must select a system that meets our specifications.

3. We have given you our specifications for the system. The system must be able to provide better information about our customers and markets.

4. We would like to have the system installed fairly quickly, perhaps within the next six months.

5. Our staff will need training. This is important. We should like to know how much assistance you can give us.

6. Obviously, there is a limit to the amount we are prepared to pay.

7. I should like to know whether your company can supply the computer system that we need.

# Individual negotiator or a team of negotiators?

Many informal negotiations are between individuals. However, some negotiations involving more complex issues, for example, international political negotiations, may be handled by a negotiating team.

individual negotiator

Consider whether you need a team of negotiators and if so, what skills are needed and what roles should they play in the negotiation? Sometimes, it is useful to have an **observer** who can take notes and a **summariser** who regularly sums up what has been agreed.

team of negotiators

## Preparing your negotiating team

These are matters that you should arrange in advance of the negotiation.

- Who will lead the discussion? (Who will make proposals and bargain? Who will summarise? Who will decide if an agreement has been reached?)

- Who will check your understanding of the other party's arguments?

- Who will check the facts of the case?

- Who will take notes?

- Who will ask questions?

- Who will answer questions from the other party?

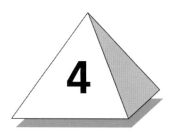

# Establishing rapport

The negotiation should not begin until everyone has been introduced to each other. In many negotiations, particularly informal negotiations, it is also important to establish rapport with the people with whom you will be negotiating. Establishing rapport helps to create a friendly and positive atmosphere for the meeting.

**ESTABLISH RAPPORT**

## What happens during this phase?

During this phase of the negotiation, you may need to use your English to do the following things:

- **Welcome** your visitors (or respond to a welcome).
- **Introduce** yourself and your colleagues.
- Use '**small talk**' to establish rapport.

## Welcome and introductions

At the beginning of the negotiation, it is usual for the host to welcome the participants and introduce people if they have not met before. In a formal meeting, the chairperson will open the discussion.

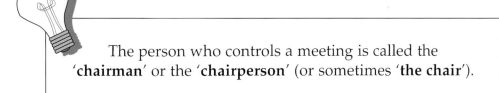

The person who controls a meeting is called the
'**chairman**' or the '**chairperson**' (or sometimes '**the chair**').

## Welcoming visitors

In formal meetings, the chairperson might welcome the visitors in one of these ways.
The visitors need not reply.

Welcome to Chadwick's.
I hope we'll have a
productive meeting
today.

**Welcome** to London,
ladies and gentlemen.

Let me begin by
welcoming you all
to Brussels.

In an informal meeting, the host might say: '**Welcome to Brussels**' or '**Welcome to Allianz**'. The visitor might respond: '**Thank you. It's a pleasure to be here**'.

## Introducing yourself and your colleagues

If you have not met the other party before, you should introduce yourself and your colleagues.

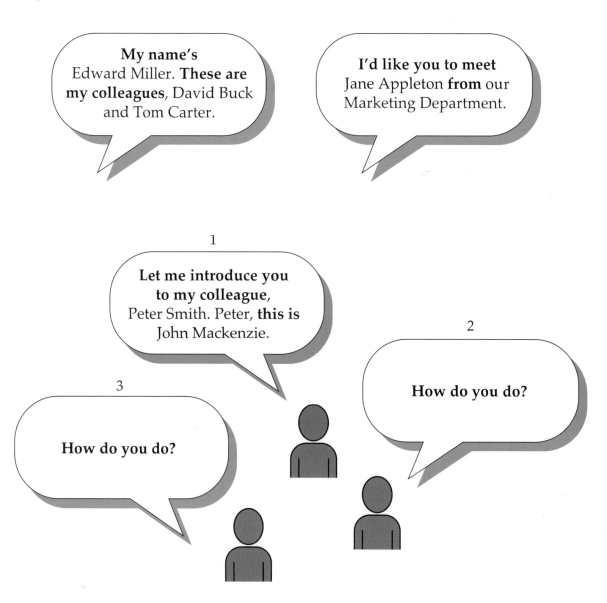

**My name's** Edward Miller. **These are my colleagues**, David Buck and Tom Carter.

**I'd like you to meet** Jane Appleton **from** our Marketing Department.

1

**Let me introduce you to my colleague**, Peter Smith. Peter, **this is** John Mackenzie.

2

How do you do?

3

How do you do?

# Establishing rapport: small talk

Before getting down to the negotiation, it is usual in most cultures to exchange 'small talk' with the other party. This helps to create a positive and friendly environment. In some cultures, it is essential to spend quite a lot of time establishing rapport.

In a formal meeting, this 'small talk' usually happens before the meeting begins and the participants have sat down at the table. You should talk about general topics and show a polite interest in what the other party says to you.

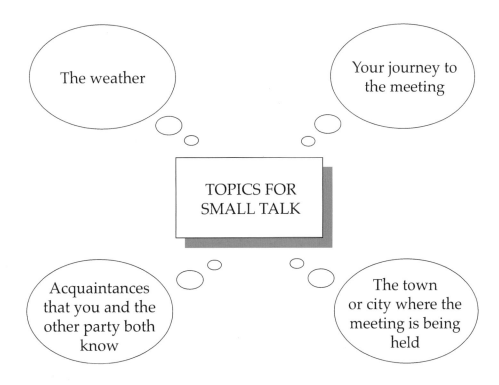

The weather

Your journey to the meeting

TOPICS FOR SMALL TALK

Acquaintances that you and the other party both know

The town or city where the meeting is being held

See Chapter 13, *Culture*.

## Examples of small talk

Here are some examples of small talk.

It is usual for the host to ask about the visitor's journey to the meeting.

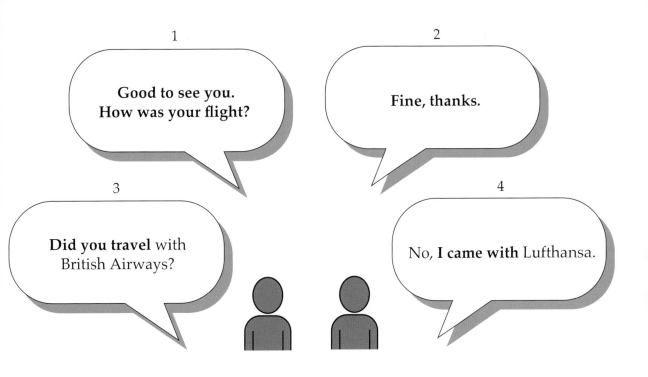

**1**
Good to see you. How was your flight?

**2**
Fine, thanks.

**3**
**Did you travel** with British Airways?

**4**
No, **I came with** Lufthansa.

**This is your first visit to** London, **isn't it? I hope you'll have a chance to see something of it while you're here.**

Yes, I hope so.

In some cultures, such as in Britain, it is usual to talk about the weather.

Occasionally, you might talk about a colleague or friend that the other party knows as well.

# Discussion: starting the negotiation

**5**

The discussion phase is the initial part of the negotiation. During this phase, you get to know more about the other party and you find out more about the other party's interests and objectives.

## The discussion phase

During this phase of the negotiation, you will need to do the following things.

- **State the purpose** of the meeting.
- **Agree an agenda** for the meeting.
- **Explain your interests** and what you hope to get from the meeting.
- **Check** that you understand correctly what the other party says to you. If you do not understand ask for **clarification**.
- Clarify any **errors of fact** or **omissions** by the other party.

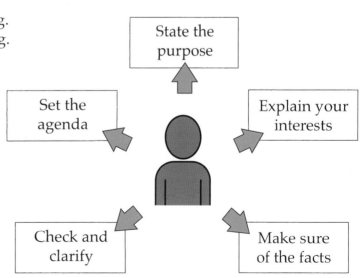

# Stating the purpose and setting the agenda

When the negotiation begins, the two parties should start by discussing their views and explaining what they hope to get out of the meeting.

A negotiation can only be effective if the two parties both know what they are discussing and why they are meeting to negotiate.

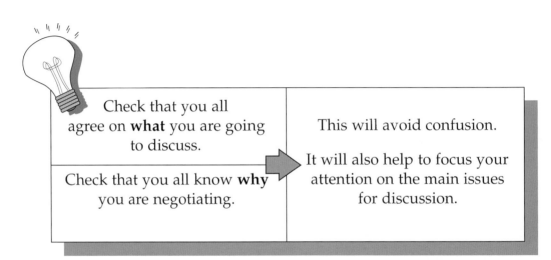

Check that you all agree on **what** you are going to discuss.

Check that you all know **why** you are negotiating.

This will avoid confusion.

It will also help to focus your attention on the main issues for discussion.

The first few minutes are very important because this is when the atmosphere of the negotiation is established.

A negotiation has a better chance of success **if the atmosphere is positive**. The two parties should be constructive and work towards an agreement. They should not think of the other party as an 'enemy' or 'opponent'.

It is helpful to agree a procedure or an agenda for the negotiation. The procedure for formal negotiations will usually be different from less formal negotiations.

| FORMAL NEGOTIATIONS | LESS FORMAL NEGOTIATIONS |
|---|---|
| There will often be a pre-set agenda for the meeting. | It is polite to come to an agreement with the other party over the procedure that you are going to follow and the order in which you will deal with various points. |

| | |
|---|---|
| Don't set the agenda yourself. | |
| Make suggestions. | You should not try to dictate the agenda. |
| Agree the agenda with the other party. | Such behaviour could annoy the other party. |

## Example

**I suggest we start by** exchanging views about the situation **and then we'll move on to** discussing how we might resolve the difficulty. **Is that acceptable to you?**

**Yes, that sounds fine.**

# Explaining your interests

Each party normally makes an opening statement. In your statement, you should:

- discuss the reasons why you are meeting the other party
- state your views on the issues concerned
- discuss your interests
- explain what you hope to achieve from the negotiation

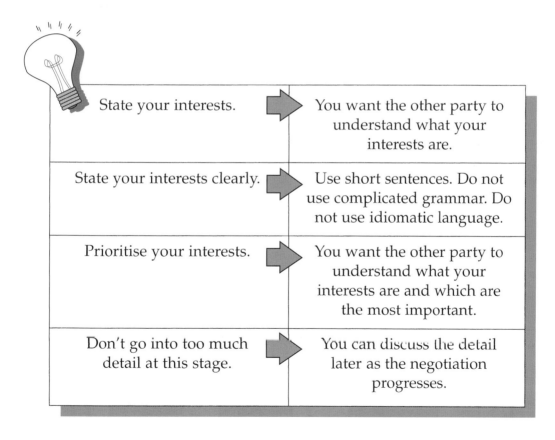

| | |
|---|---|
| State your interests. | You want the other party to understand what your interests are. |
| State your interests clearly. | Use short sentences. Do not use complicated grammar. Do not use idiomatic language. |
| Prioritise your interests. | You want the other party to understand what your interests are and which are the most important. |
| Don't go into too much detail at this stage. | You can discuss the detail later as the negotiation progresses. |

The **purpose** of this stage of the negotiation is to let the other party know what your concerns are and what you hope to achieve. You should also find out what the other party's interests are and what they are hoping to achieve.

You and the other party need to **understand** each other's interests. If neither party is unreasonable in its expectations, you should have a good basis for working towards an agreement.

See Chapter 3, *Preparation*.

When the other party is talking, listen carefully.

Don't interrupt. Wait until the other party has finished speaking before you speak yourself.

Don't talk too much. Try to talk and listen in equal proportion.

A poor negotiator talks too much and does not listen enough.

# Stating your interests

> The most important issue for us is expansion in Europe. We're particularly interested in establishing joint ventures in Central Europe with organisations such as yours.

> We're concerned about the environmental impact of your development. It is important that your planned construction programme doesn't have a damaging effect on the environment.

# Prioritising your interests

> We would eventually like to introduce a franchise operation in the Far East but it is even more important to develop the existing business in Europe.

> Our main interest is to expand our markets in the Middle East. We're also keen to improve our distribution network in Europe but this is of a lower priority at the moment.

# Checking and clarifying

Before the negotiation, you will have considered what you think the other party's likely interests will be. Now, you will find out whether you were correct. If you are not correct, you may have to change some of your planned strategies.

If there is anything you have not understood or if you are unsure whether you have understood correctly, you should ask for clarification.

Your main aim at this stage of the negotiation should be to understand each other clearly. You need to understand what the other party wants to get from the negotiation. You also need to be certain that the other party understands your interests.

Listen to the other party.

Summarise what you think he or she has said.

The other party can confirm whether your understanding is correct.

If the atmosphere is **positive**, you can work towards an agreement that satisfies **both** parties.

## Examples: checking and clarifying

There are several phrases you can use to check your understanding or to ask the other party to clarify what he or she has said.

When the other party has not understood you correctly, you should reply politely. Do not say: 'No, you are wrong'. Say instead: '**No, that's not quite right**'.

## Making sure of the facts

In some negotiations, one party might say something that is incorrect or might not be aware of something that is important to consider.

When you disagree with something the other party tells you, you should explain why you do not agree. Be friendly and positive. Do not be aggressive even when you are challenging the other party's statement.

## Errors of fact

| STATEMENT | RESPONSE |
|---|---|
| One half of the deliveries from your company in the past twelve months has been late. | I'm surprised to hear you say that. I don't think that's correct. |

## Omissions

| STATEMENT | RESPONSE |
|---|---|
| Our company has increased its sales by fifty per cent in the last two years. | Yes, that's an impressive achievement. But don't forget that your sales were very low three years ago. |

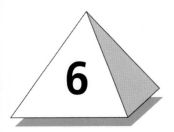

# Proposals

After the discussion phase, when you exchange information about your own and the other party's interests, you know what each party is trying to achieve from the negotiation. You should now have some idea of the obstacles to a solution. In the proposal phase of the negotiation, you should move on to finding ways to overcome the obstacles.

## What happens in the proposal phase?

During the proposal phase

- one party will **put forward a proposal.**
- the other party should **respond**. The other party might agree to the proposal, or might put forward a proposal of his or her own (a '**counter-proposal**').
- one party might indicate a willingness to make a concession by giving a **signal** by using certain words or phrases.

## Making suggestions

A proposal is a suggestion about how agreement might be reached. Proposals are '**strategic**' and are stated in broad outline. At this stage, do not concern yourself too much with the details.

When you make a proposal, you are testing the willingness of the other party to reach an agreement. You will probably begin by asking for more than you think you will get: your ideal target.

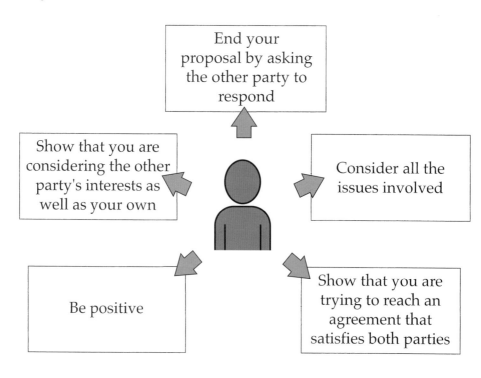

End your proposal by asking the other party to respond

Show that you are considering the other party's interests as well as your own

Consider all the issues involved

Be positive

Show that you are trying to reach an agreement that satisfies both parties

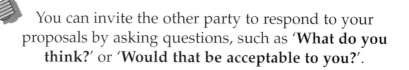

You can invite the other party to respond to your proposals by asking questions, such as '**What do you think?**' or '**Would that be acceptable to you?**'.

# Responding: counter-proposals

When one party makes a proposal, the other party must respond, sometimes by making a counter-proposal or an alternative suggestion. It may be necessary for each party to make more than one counter-proposal until an agreement in principle is reached. Skilled negotiators do not make immediate counter-proposals as these are seen as disagreement, rather than as new proposals.

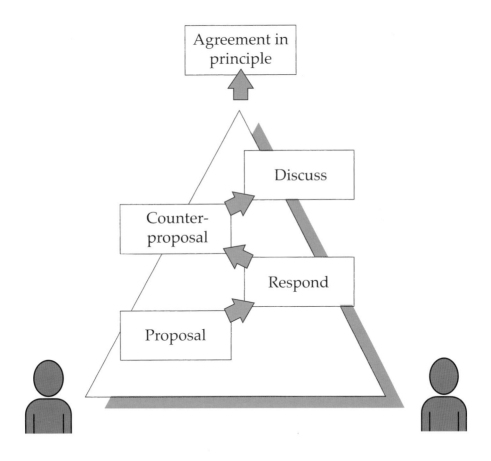

| YOU MAKE A PROPOSAL | YOU RESPOND TO A PROPOSAL |
|---|---|
| **Remain positive.** | **Remain positive.** |
| Observe the reactions of the other party carefully. **Listen carefully.** | **Do not interrupt** a proposal from the other party. **React** to the other party's proposal when they have finished speaking. |
| If the other party responds negatively, ask them to **explain why** they do not like your proposal. | The other party needs to know what you think. If you disagree, **explain why**. |

You should explain why you disagree with a proposal from the other party. This will help the other party to make a new proposal or to respond to a counter-proposal from you.

## Examples: proposing and responding to a proposal

A positive response to a proposal can sometimes lead straight to agreement without the need for bargaining. This may happen when there is only one simple issue to resolve.

You might be uncertain whether or not to agree to a proposal. Explain why you are uncertain.

You might disagree with a proposal. Explain your reasons for disagreeing.

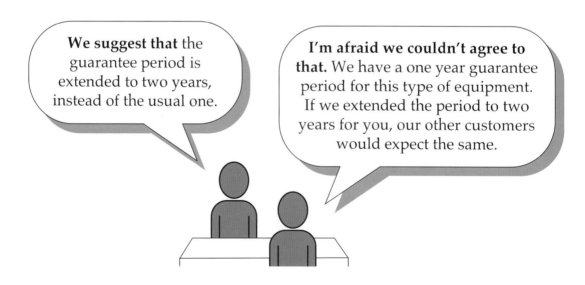

You might not agree to a proposal from the other party and put forward a suggestion of your own.

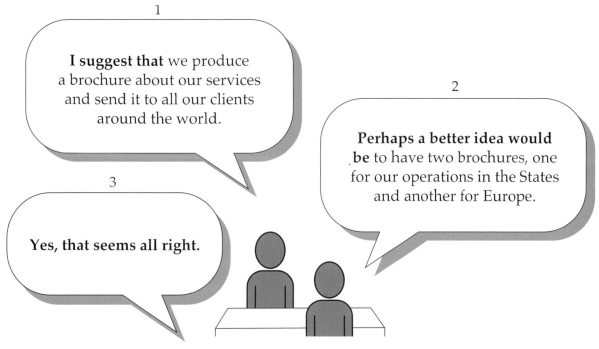

1

**I suggest that** we produce a brochure about our services and send it to all our clients around the world.

2

**Perhaps a better idea would be** to have two brochures, one for our operations in the States and another for Europe.

3

**Yes, that seems all right.**

If you cannot agree with a proposal that has been put to you, make an alternative suggestion.

**Can I make another suggestion?**

**Can I suggest something a bit different?**

## Be positive

It is important to be positive throughout a negotiation if you want to reach an agreement. Often, the **way** that you say something can be as important as **what** you say. You can say 'no' in a positive way.

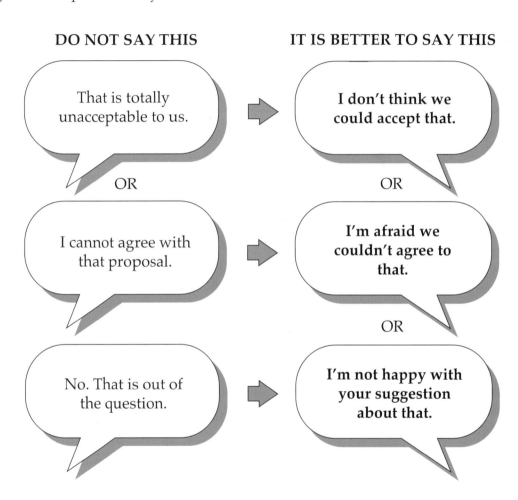

# Signals: making concessions

A '**signal**' is a verbal sign which may indicate that there is more room for negotiation over a certain issue. The other party says one thing but may be giving a signal that he or she is willing to make a concession.

Here are some examples:

| SIGNAL | INTERPRETATION | POSSIBLE REACTION |
|---|---|---|
| '**Our** NORMAL **practice is** to allow a ten per cent discount on orders of a thousand or more.' | This is their NORMAL practice, perhaps they will allow more in certain circumstances. | '**But if we** order two thousand now and another two thousand in three months time, **wouldn't you** allow us a bigger discount?' |
| 'We **don't** NORMALLY enter joint ventures.' | This is not their NORMAL practice. They might make an exception in this case. | 'But **might you be willing to make an exception** in this case? The benefits for both of us could be enormous.' |
| '**We would find it extremely** DIFFICULT to meet that deadline.' | They say it is DIFFICULT but not impossible. | '**If we agree to** pay you immediately, could you make a real effort to deliver by that date?' |

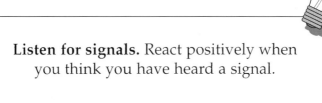

**Listen for signals.** React positively when you think you have heard a signal.

Be careful. What you think is a signal may not be one. However, it is worth asking questions to check whether it is a signal or not.

| SIGNAL | INTERPRETATION | POSSIBLE REACTION |
|---|---|---|
| 'I'M NOT SURE THAT my colleagues will be happy with that suggestion.' | But they could be persuaded if you can give some assurance. | 'If we give you a written guarantee, would that help to reassure them?' |
| OUR NORMAL delivery time is within 28 days of the order. | But if we increase our order, perhaps they will guarantee earlier delivery. | If we increase our order by 10%, could you guarantee to deliver within two weeks? |

# Signals: making your intention clear

In an international negotiation, it can be helpful to make it clear that you are going to ask a question or make a proposal, for example:

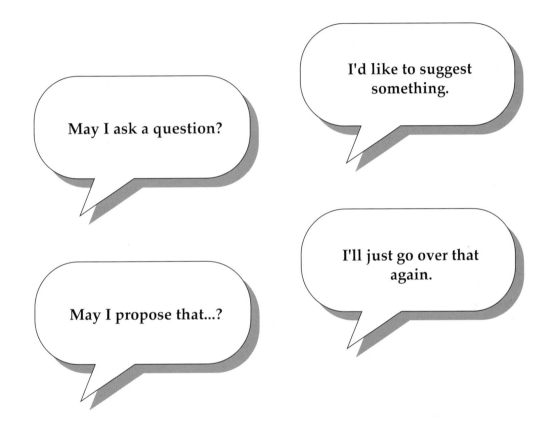

# Bargaining

In the proposing phase of a negotiation, each party gives suggestions about how an agreement might be reached. They are looking for common ground. They try to understand what the other party hopes to achieve and why.

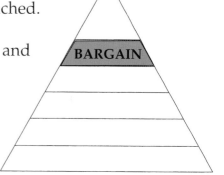

In the bargaining phase of a negotiation, each party starts to trade. It is unlikely that an agreement can be reached without some concessions from both parties.

When you bargain in English, two approaches that you might find useful are:

- linking offers to conditions
- asking hypothetical questions.

## Linking offers to conditions

When you bargain, you can link offers to conditions. You will agree to do one thing if the other party agrees to do something else. You will therefore be using **conditional language**, for example, '**If..., then...**'.

It is better to state the condition before the offer:

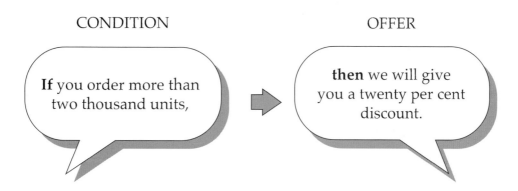

CONDITION

**If** you order more than two thousand units,

OFFER

**then** we will give you a twenty per cent discount.

This avoids interruption because the other party will want to wait until the end to see what is being offered. It is also a statement, rather than a question.

## Examples

**If you** guarantee the work for five years, **we are prepared** to accept the proposal.

**If you would be prepared to** supply us with the new machines immediately, **we might be able to** increase our offer.

**If you were prepared to** increase your offer to three million, **we could go along with that.**

## More examples

**If you were to** make a few modifications to the design, **we could** accept your offer.

**If** you **give** us a bigger discount, **then** we **will give** you the contract.

**If you gave us** a long term contract, **we would** drop the price by five per cent.

**Provided that you** can start the work immediately, **that is** acceptable to us.

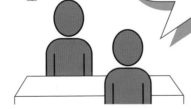

# Hypothetical questions

A hypothetical question is used to ask the other party how he or she would respond if you agree to make a concession.

A hypothetical question invites the other party to make a concession in return.

> **What if I were to** offer you more money to finish the project quickly?

You have not made any concessions yet, but you are telling the other party what concession you would make if the other party offered an acceptable concession in return.

> **What would you say if** I were to invest a million dollars in the project?

## Example

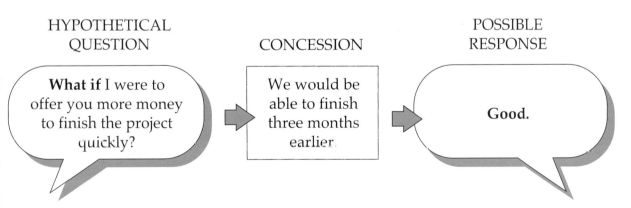

| HYPOTHETICAL QUESTION | CONCESSION | POSSIBLE RESPONSE |
| --- | --- | --- |
| **What if** I were to offer you more money to finish the project quickly? | We would be able to finish three months earlier. | **Good.** |

# Making and obtaining concessions

A concession is a change in the position that you have held in a negotiation. When you make a concession, you are offering the other party something extra. In return, you will hope to get a concession from the other party.

It is usual to **link** concessions that you give to concessions you wish to receive.

Bargaining is **trading**, not giving.

You are asking for something specific that you want and, at the same time, you are offering the other party something in return if they agree to your offer. You may have to be flexible and make some compromises at this stage.

Trade what is cheap for you but attractive for the other party.

There are several important problems with concessions.

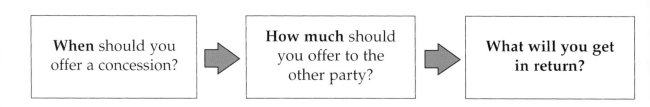

**When** should you offer a concession?

**How much** should you offer to the other party?

**What will you get in return?**

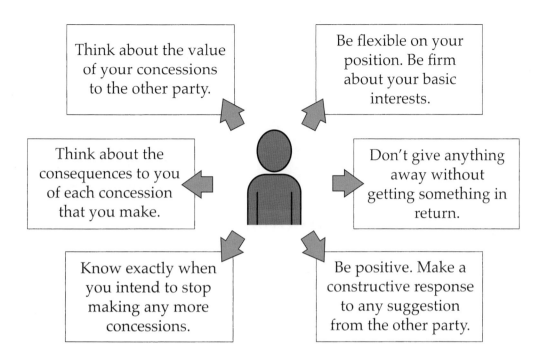

Think about the value of your concessions to the other party.

Be flexible on your position. Be firm about your basic interests.

Think about the consequences to you of each concession that you make.

Don't give anything away without getting something in return.

Know exactly when you intend to stop making any more concessions.

Be positive. Make a constructive response to any suggestion from the other party.

## Principled bargaining

The attitude of a negotiator can be described in one of three ways.

- A '**soft**' negotiator makes concessions too easily in order to reach an agreement.

- A '**hard**' negotiator is unwilling to make any concessions and tries to make the other party give in to his or her proposals.

- A '**principled**' negotiator takes into consideration the interests of the other party as well as his or her own. He or she looks for common ground and an agreement that satisfies both parties.

The terms 'soft negotiator', 'hard negotiator' and 'principled negotiator' have been used in the literature on negotiating skills by R. Fisher and W. Ury of the Harvard Negotiation Project.

| SOFT NEGOTIATOR | HARD NEGOTIATOR | PRINCIPLED NEGOTIATOR |
|---|---|---|
| Makes concessions to the other party in order to maintain a good relationship. | Demands concessions from the other party and gives little or nothing in return. | Is friendly to the other party but looks for a solution to the problem that is satisfactory to both sides. |
| Regards the other party as a friend. | Regards the other party as an opponent. | Takes the view that both parties should work together to solve a problem. |
| Wants the negotiation to end in agreement. | Wants the negotiation to end with a win. | Wants the negotiation to reach a decision that is good for both parties. |
| Changes his or her position easily. | Defends his or her position strongly. | Focuses on interests, not positions. |
| Makes offers to the other party. | Makes threats to the other party. | Discusses interests with the other party. |

| SOFT NEGOTIATOR | HARD NEGOTIATOR | PRINCIPLED NEGOTIATOR |
|---|---|---|
| Makes large concessions. | Makes no concessions, or few concessions. | Invents different ways of reaching a solution that satisfies both parties, by negotiating constructively. |
| Yields to pressure from the other party. | Applies pressure on the other party. | Uses rational discussions. He or she can be persuaded by rational argument. Does not yield to pressure from the other party. |
| Trusts the other party. | Mistrusts the other party. | Concentrates on the problem: trusting or not trusting the other party is not a important issue. |
| Agrees with what the other party says. | Insists that he or she is right. | Tries to understand the thinking of the other party. Understanding is not the same as agreeing. Understanding helps to provide a way forward to a good solution. |

A principled negotiator will usually achieve a better agreement because:

- the agreement satisfies all the parties
- it is likely to be longer lasting and more secure.

In the bargaining process, you may reject some of the suggestions put forward by the other party. The other party will probably reject some of your suggestions.

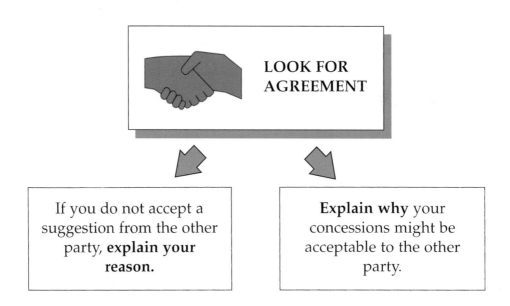

| | |
|---|---|
| If you do not accept a suggestion from the other party, **explain your reason.** | **Explain why** your concessions might be acceptable to the other party. |

It is important to be flexible and positive at all times.

# Breakdown

It is possible that you may not be able to reach agreement. For example, you might find that your interests are so far apart that agreement is not possible.

If it appears impossible to move any further, do not give up too easily. There are a number of things you can do.

Try to avoid breakdown but do not seek an agreement at all costs.

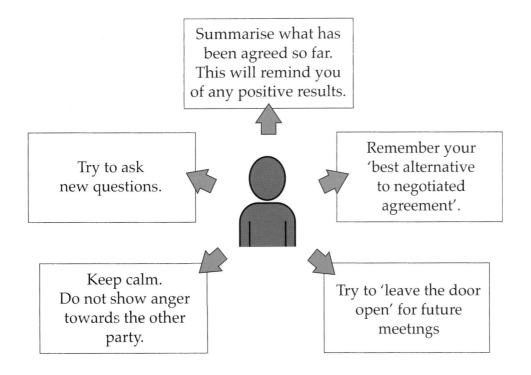

Summarise what has been agreed so far. This will remind you of any positive results.

Try to ask new questions.

Remember your 'best alternative to negotiated agreement'.

Keep calm. Do not show anger towards the other party.

Try to 'leave the door open' for future meetings

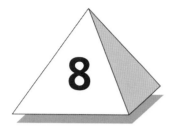

**8**

# Reaching settlement

The final stage of a successful negotiation is reaching an agreement. Each party decides that there is nothing to be gained by bargaining any further and so the bargaining ends.

## Agreement

Bargaining should not go on for longer than is necessary. If you agree with the offers put forward by the other party, **make it clear that you agree**.

SETTLE

Agreement should not be reached until:

- both parties think that they have obtained as many concessions from the other party that they can reasonably expect to win.
- both parties are satisfied with the terms and conditions on offer.

There are three important stages in reaching an effective agreement.

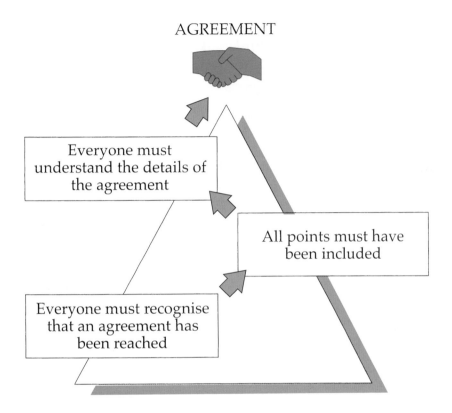

AGREEMENT

Everyone must understand the details of the agreement

All points must have been included

Everyone must recognise that an agreement has been reached

## Check that everyone is in agreement

If there is agreement over an issue, it should be clear to everyone that an agreement has been reached. Both parties should say that they agree to the proposal.

# Make sure that all points have been covered

All important points must be covered by the agreement. If they are not covered, there could be more disagreements in the future and the agreement could break down.

If you are aware of any matter that has not yet been agreed, you should bring it to the other party's attention.

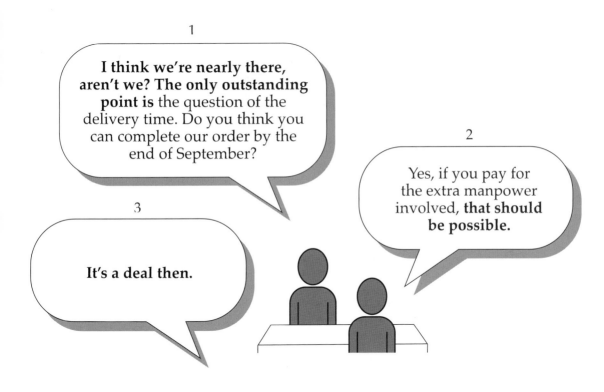

1

**I think we're nearly there, aren't we? The only outstanding point is** the question of the delivery time. Do you think you can complete our order by the end of September?

2

Yes, if you pay for the extra manpower involved, **that should be possible.**

3

**It's a deal then.**

If you think that every point has been covered, check whether the other party has any further point that he or she wishes to discuss.

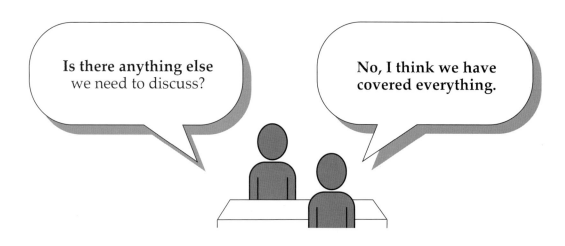

**Is there anything else** we need to discuss?

No, **I think we have covered everything.**

It might be possible to reach an agreement without covering some points, provided that these are not important. Both you and the other party can agree to meet again at a later date to discuss them.

**So, we're in agreement over all the points I've just mentioned. I'm afraid we've not come to an agreement about** the Dutch contribution to the fund. **Perhaps we can arrange another meeting to discuss the point further.**

# Understanding what has been agreed

It is essential that everyone should understand the details of the agreement and that there is no misunderstanding.

One party should summarise the agreement. The other party should reply by:

- agreeing that this summary is correct, or
- asking for something to be said again, more clearly, so as to avoid misunderstanding.

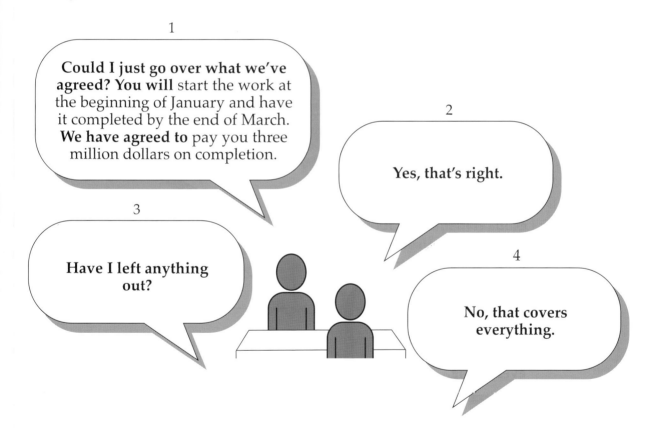

1

**Could I just go over what we've agreed? You will** start the work at the beginning of January and have it completed by the end of March. **We have agreed to** pay you three million dollars on completion.

2

**Yes, that's right.**

3

**Have I left anything out?**

4

**No, that covers everything.**

**Examples**

I'd like to thank you all for coming. I think it's been a really useful meeting. We'll send you a written summary of our agreement within a few days.

So, we'll look forward to seeing you again in March. **Thank you for coming. Goodbye.**

Thank you very much, everyone. I hope you'll have a good journey back.

## Showing a positive approach to the negotiation

Questions can be used to show the other party that you want to understand their point of view, as well as to obtain more information.

You can do this by asking questions such as:

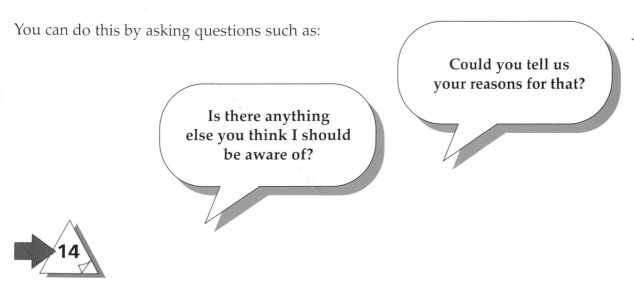

Is there anything else you think I should be aware of?

Could you tell us your reasons for that?

See Chapter 14, *Diplomatic language.*

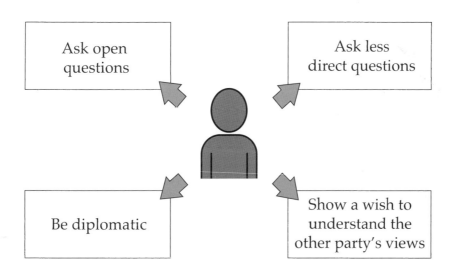

Ask open questions

Ask less direct questions

Be diplomatic

Show a wish to understand the other party's views

# Answers

You will often want to give a direct answer to questions. Sometimes, however, it can be useful to answer a question in a different way. These different ways can contribute to good negotiating technique.

|  | WHY? | EXAMPLES |
|---|---|---|
| **Avoid giving a direct answer** | You don't want to give an answer yet. You want to negotiate more. | 'Are you willing to agree to that?'<br><br>**'That would depend on various factors.'**<br><br>You can then go into different issues without really answering the question. |
| **Delay your answer** | To gain more thinking time.<br><br>To refer the question to a colleague who is not at the meeting. | **'I'd like to answer that question later, if I may.'**<br><br>**'I'm afraid I don't have that information with me at present.'**<br><br>**'I'm afraid I'd have to ask someone at Head Office for an an answer to that (question).'** |
| **Give emphasis to a point that you are making** | To tell the other party very clearly what you want to win from the negotiation. | 'Getting into the North American market **is extremely important to us.'** |

## Reacting to a negative or aggressive question

You might get a question that is negative or hostile. When this happens, the other party is indicating that an agreement is unlikely. It is important to **react positively**, to keep the negotiation moving forward.

Avoid defensive or attacking behaviour yourself. Here are some suggestions.

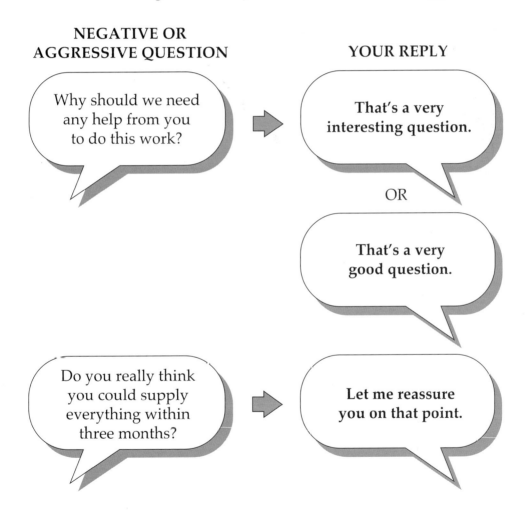

NEGATIVE OR
AGGRESSIVE QUESTION

Why should we need any help from you to do this work?

YOUR REPLY

That's a very interesting question.

OR

That's a very good question.

Do you really think you could supply everything within three months?

Let me reassure you on that point.

## Giving a vague answer

If you are asked a question that requires an answer giving an amount of money, you can use 'about' or 'approximately' to avoid saying the exact amount.

These words are also often used to talk about very large amounts of money when no one is really interested in knowing the exact amount.

For example:

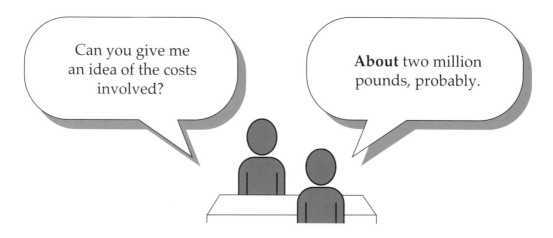

## Questions and answers

In any negotiation, each party uses questions and answers to discuss problems, bargain, make proposals and reply to proposals. Here are some examples.

## PROBING QUESTION

**I wonder if you can tell us** a little more about your plans for expanding into Central Europe. Are you planning to set up subsidiaries or agencies?

## AVOIDING A DIRECT ANSWER

**I'm afraid I can't give you an answer to that question at the moment.** We haven't decided yet.

## OPEN QUESTION

**How important is** the time factor to you?

## GIVING EMPHASIS TO YOUR REPLY

Well, **it's vital that** we receive all the components by the end of March at the latest.

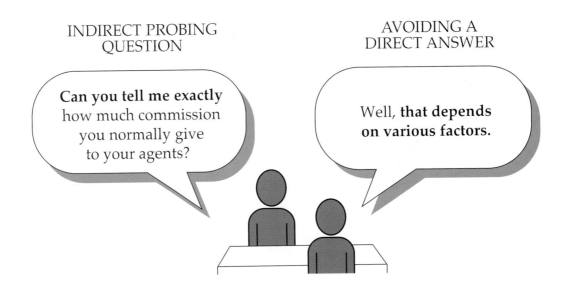

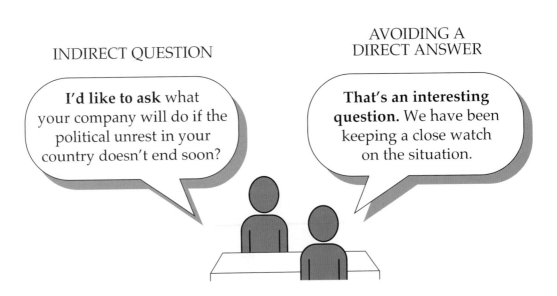

NEGATIVE QUESTION

**Don't you think that** opening a new factory in the Far East will result in many redundancies in your factories in Europe?

ANSWERING POSITIVELY

**You don't need to worry about that.** We don't anticipate that many jobs will be lost.

NEGATIVE STATEMENT

I think that our companies have completely different objectives.

BEING DIPLOMATIC

**I'm not sure that I understand you properly.** Could you explain a bit further?

# Part Two: Approach

# Approaches to the negotiation

**10**

When you negotiate, your aim is to reach a satisfactory agreement with the other party. Creating a positive negotiating climate will help you to do this.

Creating a positive negotiating climate involves establishing rapport with the other party, being diplomatic and thinking about how you will handle any problems which arise.

See Chapter 12, *Rapport,* Chapter 14, *Diplomatic language*, and Chapter 15, *Handling problems.*

You should also be aware of body language and of any cultural differences that might exist between you and the other party. For example, negotiating in western cultures may be very different from negotiating in eastern cultures.

See Chapter 11, *Body language*, and Chapter 13, *Culture.*

# Your approach to the negotiation

A skilled negotiator always considers these aspects of behaviour when negotiating.

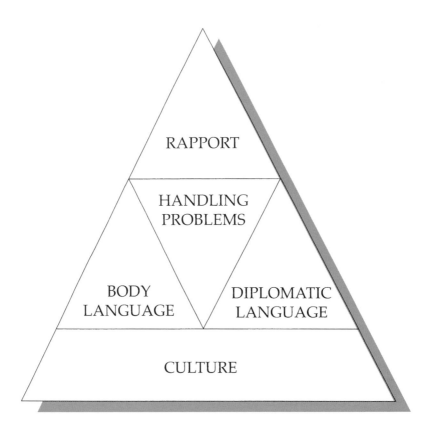

# Body language

Some people believe that you can understand another person's attitudes and feelings by detecting signals given by the body. Looking at these signals can help you to build up a picture and to gain an overall impression.

Body language can be important in negotiations. It can help you to understand the other person better.

For example, you might be able to see by looking at the way someone is sitting or moving parts of his or her body, that he or she is or is not interested in something.

Here are some examples of body language:

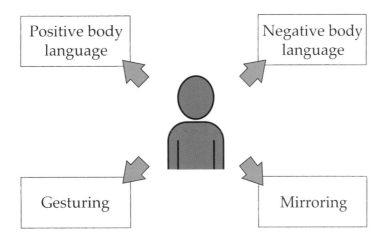

# Positive and negative body language

Body language may differ between cultures. There are some aspects of body language that, in **western cultures**, are generally recognised as being positive, and some aspects of body language that are negative.

## Positive body language

**Positive** body language shows that a person has a positive attitude to the negotiation. He or she is interested in the discussion and is looking for a way to reach agreement.

| THE OTHER PERSON... | IT MAY MEAN... |
|---|---|
| Leans forward when listening to you. | The person is interested in what you are saying. |
| Maintains eye contact with you, both when speaking and listening to you. | The person is interested or that they are telling the truth. |
| Sits upright. | The person is confident and interested. |
| Uses relaxed gestures. | The person is confident. |

# Negative body language

**Negative** body language shows that a person is not interested in reaching an agreement. He or she does not want to listen to the other party and does not expect to reach an agreement. The person could be aggressive or uninterested.

| THE OTHER PERSON... | IT MAY MEAN... |
|---|---|
| Looks down and does not look at you. | The person is not interested in the discussion. |
| Folds arms across his or her chest, and sits upright or leans backwards. | The person is defensive and may not like what you are saying. |
| Clenches his or her fists. | The person is defensive or frustrated. |
| Covers his or her mouth with hands. | The person is nervous or is not telling the truth. |
| Looks at watch or clock. | The person is bored. |

In **some eastern cultures**, when a person looks down and not **at** you, he or she is doing this as a sign of respect.

## Gestures

When a person gets excited or feels very strongly about something, he or she might use exaggerated gestures.

Examples of exaggerated gestures include:

- waving your arm(s) in the air
- pointing at something with your finger
- hitting the table with your fist.

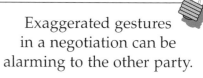

Exaggerated gestures
in a negotiation can be
alarming to the other party.

**Try to avoid them.**

## Mirroring

Sometimes, when two people are talking to each other, one of them might copy the body movements or body positions of the other person. We call this 'mirroring'. Leaning forward when the other person leans forward is an example.

Many people believe that mirroring is a signal that the other person wants to be friendly and wants to have a positive negotiating environment.

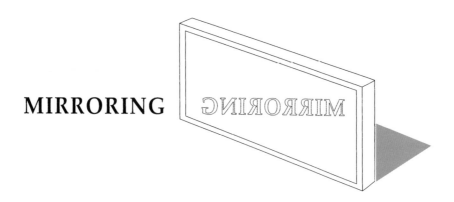

# Should you control your body language?

It is useful to be aware of body language and what it means.

It is **not** sensible to change your own behaviour deliberately in an attempt to give a message to the other person. Try to act naturally.

Body language can be difficult to understand properly. It is certainly helpful to be aware of body language signals but it is also worth considering that you may be wrong in your interpretation.

| DO! | DON'T! |
|---|---|
| **Be aware of your own body language.**<br><br>**Consider what message you are giving to the other party.** | Don't use any exaggerated gestures.<br><br>Don't use any gestures or body language that may be offensive in the culture in which you are negotiating. |

In an international negotiation, the signals given by people from another culture may not have the same meaning as in your culture. For example, nodding the head (up and down) usually means agreement in western cultures and shaking the head from right to left means disagreement. In some other cultures, these body movements can have exactly the opposite meaning!

If you are going to negotiate with people from a completely different culture, it is sensible to find out about any potential differences in body language.

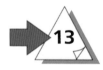

See Chapter 13, *Culture*.

# Rapport

**12**

'Rapport' means sympathetic understanding between people. Communication is a vital part of negotiation. Without rapport, communication is less effective and it breaks down.

If you build rapport with the other party, you will create a positive negotiating climate and may reach an agreement more quickly.

Building rapport is particularly important in international negotiations, where misunderstandings may occur because of language and cultural differences. If the rapport is good between the negotiating parties, mistakes will be forgiven and misunderstandings will be less frequent.

# How to build rapport

Here are some useful ways to establish rapport:

- make 'small talk' before and after the negotiation and during any breaks
- show interest in the other party's point of view
- make it clear that you are taking their interests into consideration when you make proposals and bargain
- remain positive. If the other party is negative, try to find out why by asking questions
- use positive body language
- do not do anything which may offend people from another culture.

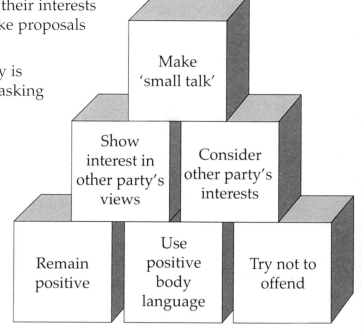

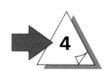

See Chapter 4, *Establishing rapport*.

See Chapter 11, *Body language*.

## Language

Your choice of language can also affect your relationship with the other party. It is important not to be too blunt. You should use tactful language.

See Chapter 14, *Diplomatic language*.

## Signal your behaviour

You can give the other party signals about what you intend to do next. This is particularly important in an international negotiation when the other party might not understand you easily.

**Signalling behaviour**

- makes it clear to the other party what you are doing
- encourages them to listen to what you are going to say.

# Examples of behaviour signalling

I'd just like to check something.

May I ask a question?

Can I clarify something?

Can I make a suggestion?

I'd like to summarise what we've agreed so far.

# Avoid irritating comments

You should avoid comments that irritate the other party. When negotiators make a lot of positive comments about how good their offers are, for example, this can be very irritating to the other party who should be able to decide for themselves what they think about the offer. They do not want to be told what to think.

Being personal and making negative comments about the other party is also annoying.

You can irritate people in various ways. For example, **do not say**:

- 'You don't have enough experience to know...'
- 'I have much more experience than you...'
- 'I don't see the point of this.'
- 'I'm not interested.'

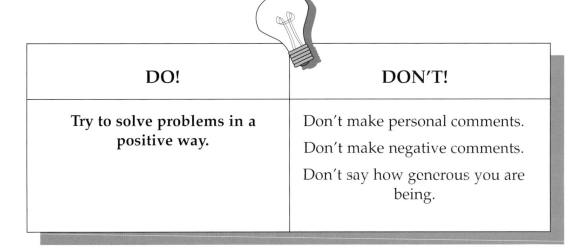

| DO! | DON'T! |
| :---: | :---: |
| **Try to solve problems in a positive way.** | Don't make personal comments. Don't make negative comments. Don't say how generous you are being. |

# Avoid threatening behaviour

If you threaten or attack the other party, they will become defensive. Criticism, for example, is a form of attack and it encourages the recipients to defend themselves. This defence also looks like an attack and so the behaviour continues and becomes rather like a spiral.

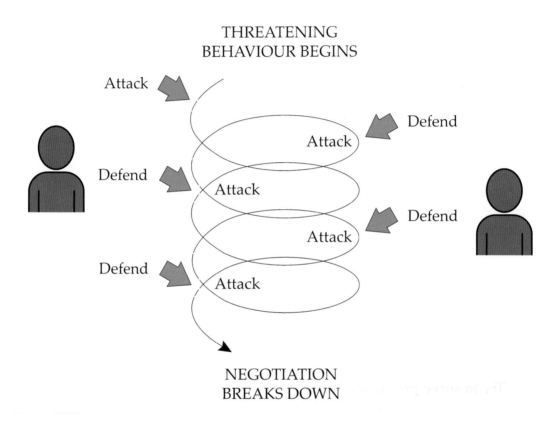

# Culture

People from different cultures may negotiate in different ways. If they do, you ought to be aware of what those differences are.

## Why is cultural awareness important?

Many business deals have gone wrong and a great deal of money has been wasted as a result of a lack of cultural awareness in international negotiations.

Through ignorance of cultural differences, you may:

- fail to win the respect of the people you are negotiating with
- misinterpret their behaviour
- cause unintentional offence by doing something that is offensive to people from another culture.

This may cause a breakdown in the negotiation.

It is dangerous to have a fixed idea of stereotypes. You should carefully research into the cultural background of the other party before the negotiation.

**Observation** during the negotiation is as important as research beforehand. **Observe** what other people do.

Don't expect everyone from one culture to behave in the same way. We are all individuals!

You may wish to make a note of aspects of the cultural background of people you negotiate with. You can learn about these from colleagues or from your own experience.

Here are some areas to consider before you negotiate with people from other cultural backgrounds.

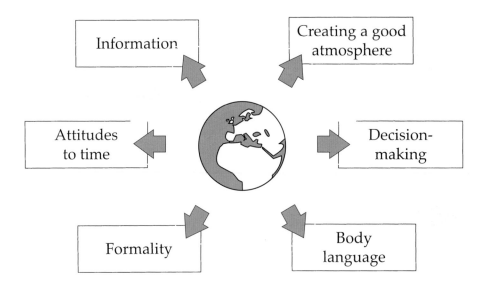

# Creating a good atmosphere

For people from some cultural backgrounds, it is very important to create a good atmosphere before the negotiations begin. This helps to create trust and rapport between the parties.

A good atmosphere can be created by spending as much time as possible on **'small talk'** when the parties first meet.

You may cause offence by trying to get down to business too quickly.

| HOW TO CREATE A GOOD ATMOSPHERE | |
|---|---|
| Have you met the other person before?<br><br>**Yes** ➡ Talk about that meeting.<br><br>**No** ➡ Explain where you come from, your job, and your company and its business. | Most cultures |
| Are you meeting in the other person's country?<br><br>**Yes** ➡ Talk about what you have seen or would like to see there. | Most cultures |

You can use the space in the boxes below to make notes about aspects of the cultural background of those you are going to negotiate with.

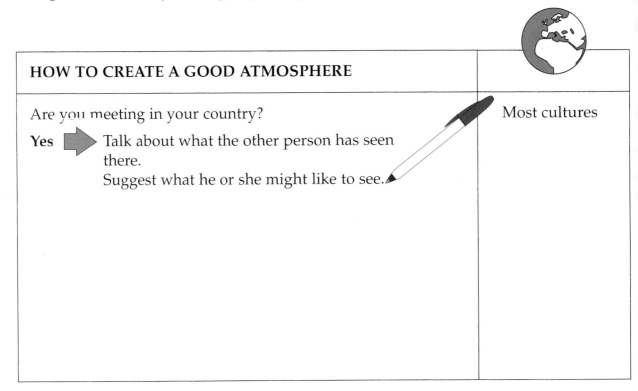

**HOW TO CREATE A GOOD ATMOSPHERE**

Are you meeting in your country?                                          Most cultures

**Yes** ➡ Talk about what the other person has seen there.
Suggest what he or she might like to see.

## Decision-making

In many cultures, negotiatiors expect to reach an agreement when they meet and to 'shake hands on a deal'. In other cultures, things are done differently.

- Decisions are rarely taken during the meeting to negotiate.
- A report is taken back to the negotiator's senior colleagues at head office. The senior colleagues then make the decision.
- Senior or elderly colleagues may attend a negotiation meeting but only to observe, not to participate.

In some cultures, an initial meeting may be held just to 'test the water' - to see what the atmosphere is like and to find out whether there is good rapport with the other party. In the initial meeting, they do not expect to make any serious decisions.

| THINGS TO REMEMBER ABOUT DECISION-MAKING | |
|---|---|
| The other party may expect to reach an agreement at the meeting and to 'shake hands on a deal'. | United States |

# Information

In some cultures, negotiators expect to provide the other party with a large amount of information that may be useful. They come to the negotiation with documents to give to the other party.

In other cultures, negotiators provide less information or less detailed information. They will often be willing to give you the information you need but only if you ask for it.

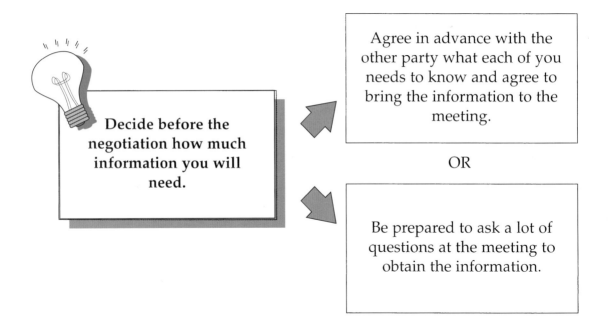

**Decide before the negotiation how much information you will need.**

Agree in advance with the other party what each of you needs to know and agree to bring the information to the meeting.

OR

Be prepared to ask a lot of questions at the meeting to obtain the information.

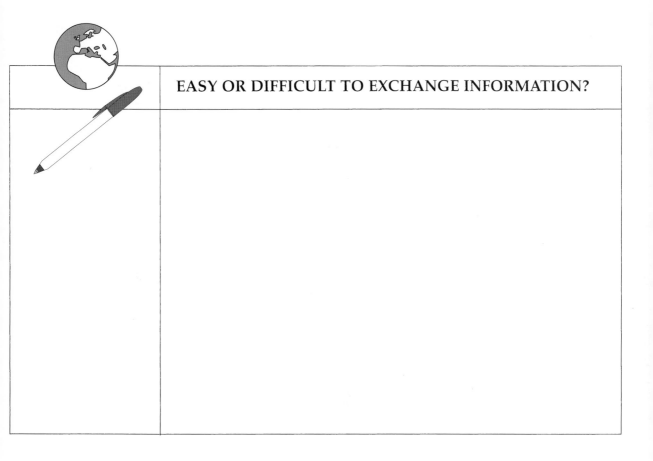

| | **EASY OR DIFFICULT TO EXCHANGE INFORMATION?** |
|---|---|
| | |

## Attitudes to time

People in different cultures have different attitudes to time. In some cultures, it is the normal custom to start meetings punctually, at the exact time agreed. In other cultures, punctuality is not so important. Often, meetings will start much later than planned.

In some cultures, people deal with more than one thing at a time. They will accept an interruption to a business meeting if some other matter needs attending to.

| | ATTITUDE TO TIME |
|---|---|
| Germany | Meetings always start on time. |

## Formality

In some cultures, people are very formal when they meet, particularly when they meet at work. In other cultures, informality is more acceptable.

It is important that both parties in a negotiation should be comfortable about the degree of formality or informality between them.

| CONSIDER... | |
|---|---|
| **Forms of address** | Do you use first names, or titles and surnames? Is it **Peter** or **Mr Smith**? Does any person in the other party's negotiating team expect to be addressed in a particular way? For example, **Doctor** Schmidt? |
| **Clothes** | What clothes should be worn at the meeting? **Men** Should it be a dark suit and tie or something different? **Women** Should it be a formal two-piece suit? What about the length of hemline, sleeves or neckline? |
| **Business cards** | In some cultures, you will expect to exchange business cards when you meet. |
| **Socialising** | Are there particular customs to be aware of when you socialise with the other party's negotiators? |
| **Relationship between superiors and their subordinates** | In some cultures, junior officials or managers are required to treat their superiors with great respect and formality. In other cultures, less importance is placed on differences in seniority during a business meeting: each person may be allowed to contribute freely to the discussion. |
| **Use of formal and diplomatic language** | Where formality is important, you must expect to use more formal and diplomatic language. |

| | **THINGS TO REMEMBER ABOUT FORMALITY OR INFORMALITY** |
|---|---|
| Japan | Exchange business cards when you meet. |

# Body language

In some cultures, negotiators are very interested in watching the reactions, body language and manners of the other party's negotiators. They can be less concerned with the verbalisation of facts. This can be important when they are meeting for the first time.

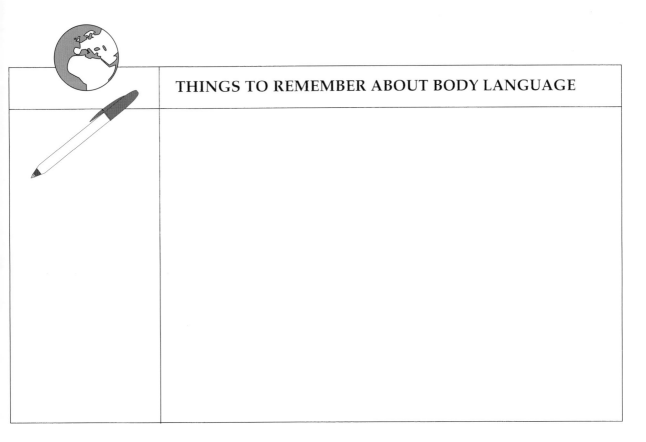

**THINGS TO REMEMBER ABOUT BODY LANGUAGE**

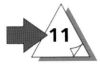

See Chapter 11, *Body language*.

# Diplomatic language

**14**

A skillful negotiator uses diplomatic language. In a negotiation, how you express your ideas and opinions can be important.

Try to use diplomatic language. For example:

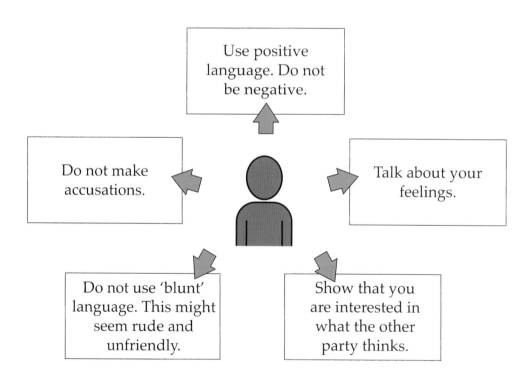

Use positive language. Do not be negative.

Do not make accusations.

Talk about your feelings.

Do not use 'blunt' language. This might seem rude and unfriendly.

Show that you are interested in what the other party thinks.

# Use positive language

When you negotiate, you should be looking for an agreement that satisfies the interests of all the parties. In order to move towards an agreement, it can be important to

- use positive language
- avoid negative language.

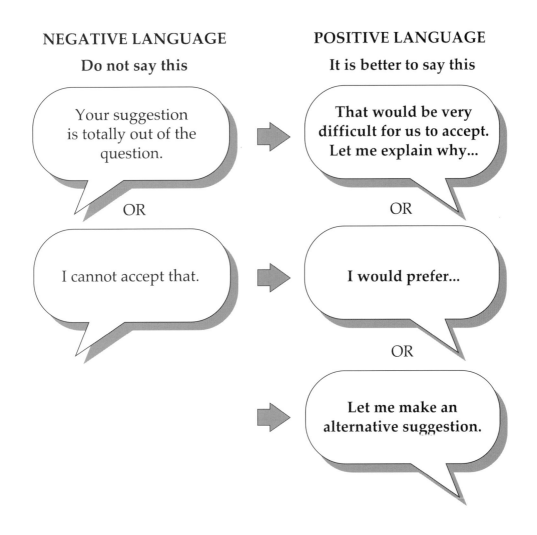

**NEGATIVE LANGUAGE**
**Do not say this**

**POSITIVE LANGUAGE**
**It is better to say this**

Your suggestion is totally out of the question.

That would be very difficult for us to accept. Let me explain why...

OR

OR

I cannot accept that.

I would prefer...

OR

Let me make an alternative suggestion.

You should encourage the other party to move towards your position or make suggestions as to how an agreement can be reached.

## Do not use 'blunt' language

'Blunt' language is language that is too direct and not tactful. It is used by someone who likes to state opinions regardless of the effect the words are having on the listener. Blunt language, coming from a person you do not know very well, is usually rude and offensive.

A person who **uses** blunt language may not intend to be rude and offensive.

A person who **hears** blunt language (who is spoken to 'bluntly') will usually feel angry or irritated.

It is very easy to use blunt language without knowing that this is what you are doing.

Here are some examples of blunt language and also of a better (more diplomatic) way to say the same thing.

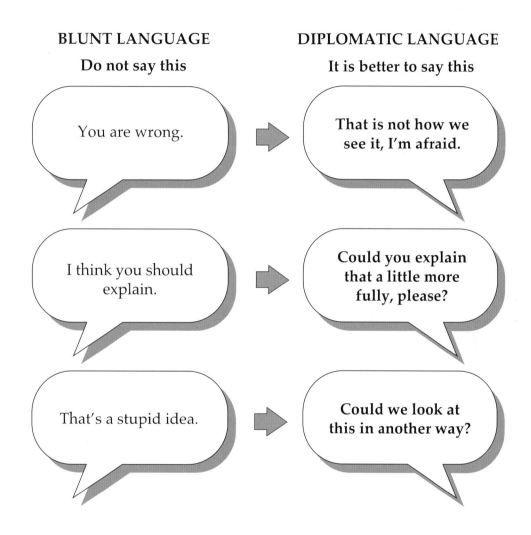

| BLUNT LANGUAGE | DIPLOMATIC LANGUAGE |
| --- | --- |
| **Do not say this** | **It is better to say this** |

You are wrong. → **That is not how we see it, I'm afraid.**

I think you should explain. → **Could you explain that a little more fully, please?**

That's a stupid idea. → **Could we look at this in another way?**

## Asking for clarification

If the other party uses vague language and you do not understand what they are saying, you may want to move the negotiation forward.

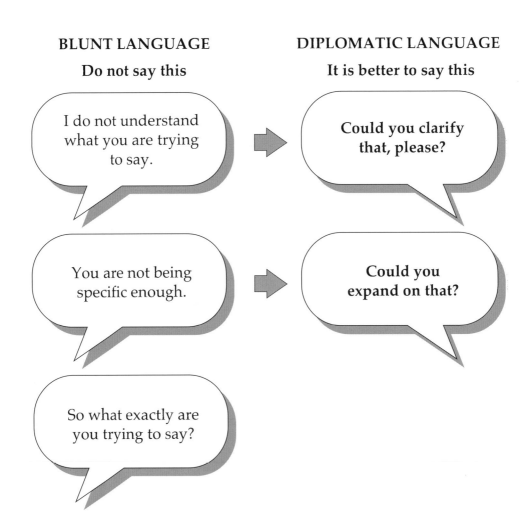

**BLUNT LANGUAGE**
**Do not say this**

I do not understand what you are trying to say.

You are not being specific enough.

So what exactly are you trying to say?

**DIPLOMATIC LANGUAGE**
**It is better to say this**

**Could you clarify that, please?**

**Could you expand on that?**

# Do not make accusations

Do not speak in a way that makes it seem that you are accusing the other party of doing something wrong.

## Examples

You might be confused by what the other party says to you. Do not accuse the other party of confusing you.

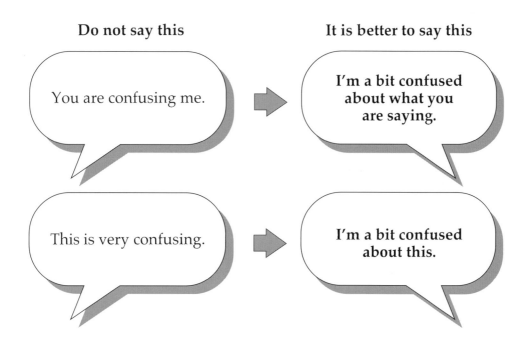

**Do not say this**

You are confusing me.

**It is better to say this**

**I'm a bit confused about what you are saying.**

This is very confusing.

**I'm a bit confused about this.**

You might be worried by something the other party says or proposes. Do not accuse the other party of worrying you deliberately.

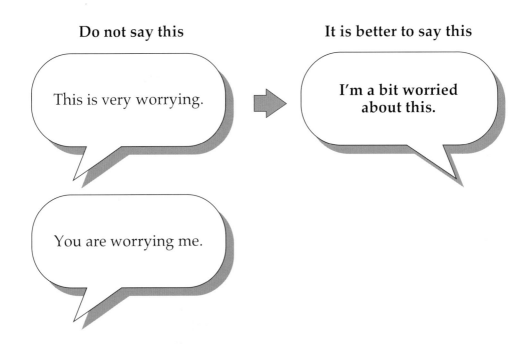

| **Do not say this** | | **It is better to say this** |
| --- | --- | --- |

This is very worrying.

I'm a bit worried about this.

You are worrying me.

## Show interest in what the other party thinks

A negotiator must always show interest in what the other party thinks and what the other party would like to happen.

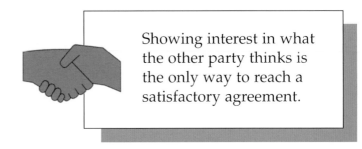

Showing interest in what the other party thinks is the only way to reach a satisfactory agreement.

**Diplomatic language** can be used to show the other party that you are interested in what they would like or what they think. For example:

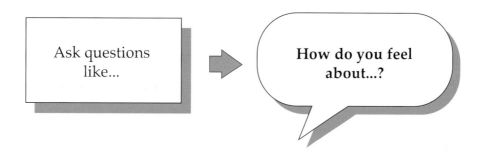

## Help the other party to imagine an outcome

You can do this by making suggestions and asking for opinions. For example:

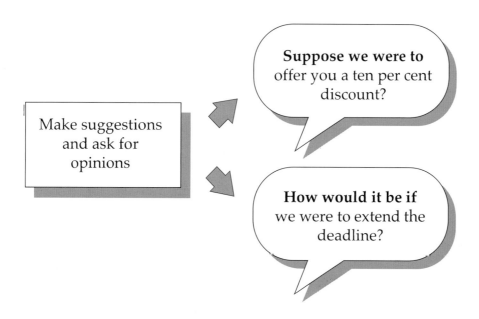

Other phrases you can use are:

What would happen if...?

What if we were to...?

## Talk about your feelings

In a negotiation, it is important not to be emotional. On the other hand, if you are pleased, surprised or shocked by something the other party has done, be open about how you feel. Use diplomatic language to express your feelings, for example:

I am a little surprised that...

I am pleased you agree with this.

# Handling problems

**15**

Negotiating is not easy. The parties begin with different ideas about what the outcome should be. The skill of a negotiator is to look for common ground and a solution that is satisfactory to everyone.

## Why do problems occur?

There will often be a strong difference of opinion in negotiation. Sometimes there may be a danger of **conflict** arising.

Conflict can arise for several reasons.

- Lack of trust
- Misunderstanding
- Different objectives
- Competition.

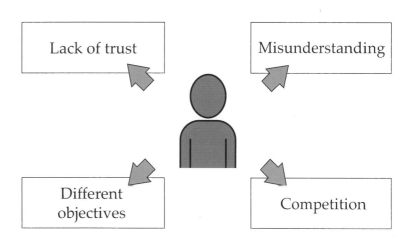

# Successful negotiation: handling conflict

Think about solving any problems which may arise.

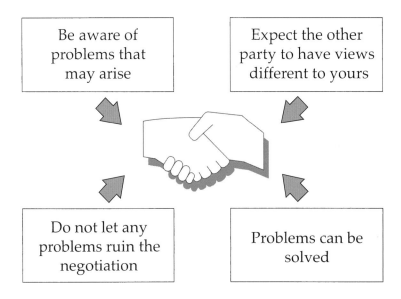

| | |
|---|---|
| Be aware of problems that may arise | Expect the other party to have views different to yours |
| Do not let any problems ruin the negotiation | Problems can be solved |

During many negotiations, there is a critical time when the talks are in danger of breaking down. There is conflict between the parties.

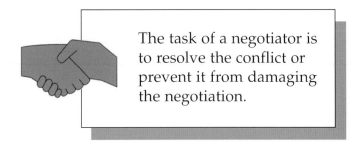

The task of a negotiator is to resolve the conflict or prevent it from damaging the negotiation.

# Avoiding conflict: dealing with lack of trust

There might be a lack of trust between you and the other party. A lack of trust might exist:

- when you do not know the people you are talking to
- because of cultural differences between you and the other party.

| BEFORE THE NEGOTIATION | DURING THE NEGOTIATION |
|:---:|:---:|
| Research into possible cultural differences. | Be open. Be willing to express your feelings and your concerns. |

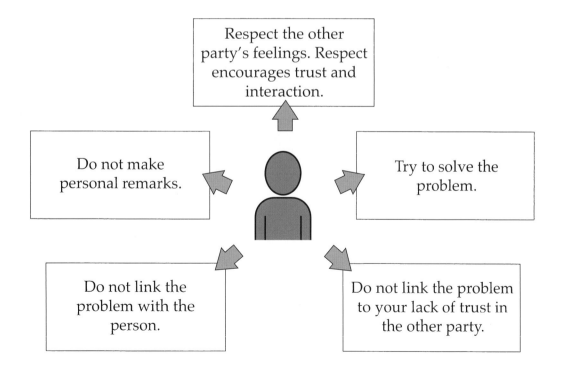

# Avoiding conflict: dealing with misunderstanding

Conflict can arise because

- the other person does not properly understand what you are saying, or
- you do not understand what the other person is saying.

This happens in negotiations between two people from the same country. It is much more common when two people from different countries and cultures are negotiating. Understanding a foreign language properly can be very difficult.

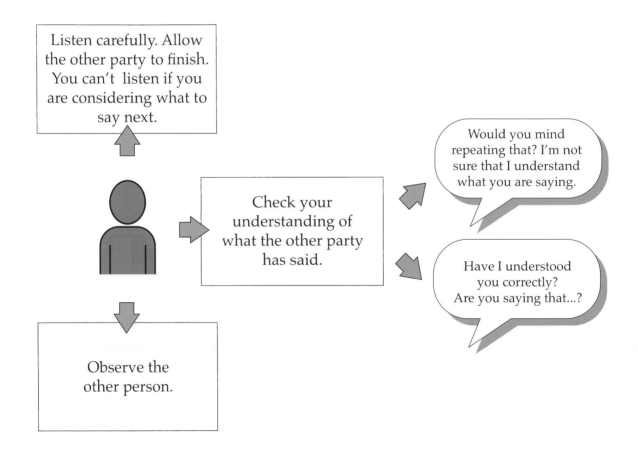

# Avoiding conflict: dealing with different objectives

Your objectives will differ from the objectives of the other party. That is why people negotiate - to try to find solutions.

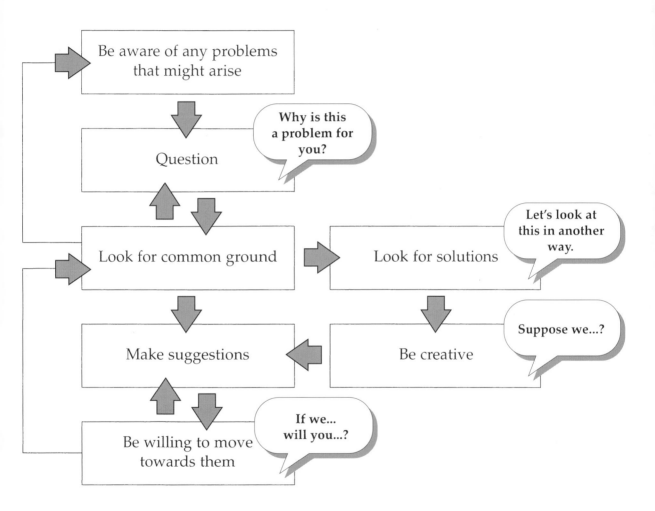

# Avoiding conflict: dealing with competition

Finding a solution to a problem can be very difficult when the parties see themselves as competitors. It is easy for competitors to get into conflict.

Remember that you are meeting to negotiate.

Both parties will be looking for a solution to the problem.

USE YOUR NEGOTIATING SKILLS

If you think they are trying to trick you, you should **challenge** what they are saying. Make it clear that you know it is a trick.

**Do not become aggressive.**

**Question** what they are saying.

**Do not give in to threats.**

**Remain calm** and try to keep to a **problem-solving** approach.

# Dealing with breakdown

Sometimes, negotiations break down and it seems impossible to make any progress. If this happens, what should you do?

## Adjournments

- Ask for a short break
- Use the break to discuss the problem with the rest of your team.
- Analyse what might have caused the break-down.

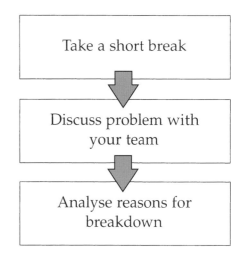

## When the talks resume

- Summarise everything that has been agreed so far.
- Summarise the reasons for the disagreement that threatens to end the negotiation.
- Talk openly about the consequences of not reaching agreement

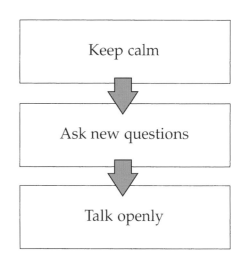

# What will happen if you cannot agree?

How important is an agreement to both parties?

Always be aware of your BATNA.

You can tell the other party what you will do if you can't reach your agreement.

> If we can't reach an agreement, we shall cancel our order.

> You don't leave me any choice. I shall have to dismiss some of our staff.

!

**Remember:** You want something better than your BATNA. So does the other party. Keep looking for a solution.

AT ALL TIMES
BE POSITIVE!

# Part Three: Evaluation

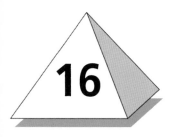

# **Preparing for a negotiation**

**16**

Answer the questions in this checklist before you start a negotiation. Your answers will help you to think about whether your preparation for the negotiation has been satisfactory.

## Preparation checklist

PREPARATION CHECKLIST

**My objectives**

|   |   | Yes | No |
|---|---|---|---|
| 1. | Have I identified my objectives? | ☐ | ☐ |
| 2. | Have I put my objectives in order of importance (in order of priority)? | ☐ | ☐ |
| 3. | Have I decided which of these objectives I must achieve? | ☐ | ☐ |

## PREPARATION CHECKLIST

**My objectives** (continued)

|  |  | Yes | No |
|---|---|---|---|

4. Have I decided which of these objectives I hope to achieve?
   (These are objectives that you wish to achieve if the negotiation goes well, but you will not refuse to reach an agreement if you do not achieve them.)

5. Have I decided which of these objectives I would like to achieve but are of less importance for the negotiation?
   (If I achieve these objectives, I will be more successful than I expect to be.)

**BATNA**

6. Do I know what will happen if we do not reach an agreement?

7. Have I identified my **best alternative to negotiated agreement** (BATNA)?
   (See page 14.)

## PREPARATION CHECKLIST

**Information**                                    Yes    No

8.  Have I obtained all the information that may be    ☐      ☐
    necessary to put forward my arguments?

**The other party**

9.  Do I know the other party (the person I will be    ☐      ☐
    meeting for the negotiation)?

10. (If the answer to Question 9 is 'No', answer this
    question.)
    Can I find out more about the other party?         ☐      ☐

    For example:    Who is he or she?
                    What is his or her position?
                    What is his or her experience?

11. What is the nationality of the other party?        ☐      ☐

12. Are there likely to be cultural differences?       ☐      ☐
    (See pages 144-148 for a cross-cultural
    questionnaire.)

## PREPARATION CHECKLIST

**The other party** (continued)                                    Yes      No

    13.  Have I considered the **interests** of the other party?

    14.  Have I considered the **position** that the other party might take at the start of the negotiation?

**Reaching agreement**

    15.  Have I considered how I might persuade the other party to move towards my position?

    16.  Have I considered the reasons why the other party might disagree with my proposals?

    17.  Have I identified **common ground** that we share?

    18.  Have I considered **possible compromises** for reaching agreement?

# Vocabulary

If you are negotiating in a foreign language, it is easy to forget important words or phrases when you need them.

VOCABULARY

Use this page to make a list of words and phrases that you might use.

(There is no need to write words that are familiar to you. Write down words or phrases that you might forget!)

## VOCABULARY

# VOCABULARY

# Cross-cultural checklist

You can use this checklist to help you prepare for a negotiation with people from a different culture. Before you think about the other party, it is useful to consider how things are done in your own culture and then to consider possible differences.

---

CROSS-CULTURAL CHECKLIST

---

**Creating a good atmosphere**

|  | Yes | Fairly important | No |
|---|---|---|---|
| Is it important to spend a lot of time on small talk? | ☐ | ☐ | ☐ |
| In my country, do we like to get down to business quickly? | ☐ | ☐ | ☐ |

---

# CROSS-CULTURAL CHECKLIST

**Formality**

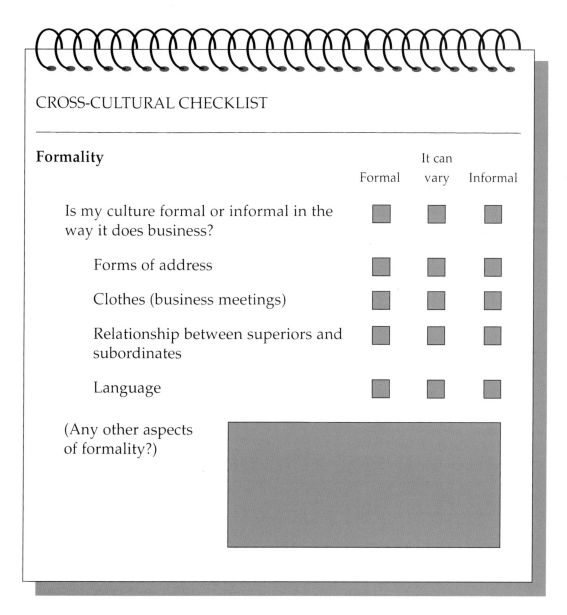

|  | Formal | It can vary | Informal |
|---|---|---|---|
| Is my culture formal or informal in the way it does business? | ☐ | ☐ | ☐ |
| Forms of address | ☐ | ☐ | ☐ |
| Clothes (business meetings) | ☐ | ☐ | ☐ |
| Relationship between superiors and subordinates | ☐ | ☐ | ☐ |
| Language | ☐ | ☐ | ☐ |

(Any other aspects of formality?)

## CROSS-CULTURAL CHECKLIST

| **Shaking hands** | Yes | It varies | No |
|---|---|---|---|
| Is it usual in my culture to shake hands with someone when we meet? |  |  |  |

| **Humour** | Yes | It depends | No |
|---|---|---|---|
| Is humour acceptable in business meetings in my country? |  |  |  |

| **Exchange of information** | Yes | It can vary | No |
|---|---|---|---|
| Is it usual in my culture to exchange information freely without having to be asked for it by the other party? |  | | |

| | Yes | Sometimes | No |
|---|---|---|---|
| Would I accept interruptions, such as telephone calls, during a negotiation meeting? |  |  | |

# CROSS-CULTURAL CHECKLIST

|  | Yes | Sometimes | No |
|---|---|---|---|
| Am I expected to arrive on time for a meeting? | ☐ | ☐ | ☐ |
| Is it usual in my country to reach an agreement in meetings? | ☐ | ☐ | ☐ |
| Is it usual in my country to consult with superiors or colleagues later, after the meeting, before reaching an agreement? | ☐ | ☐ | ☐ |
| Is body language considered important in my country? | ☐ | ☐ | ☐ |

What gestures or body language are regarded as positive?

NOW THINK ABOUT ALL THESE QUESTIONS AGAIN IN RELATION TO THE CULTURAL BACKGROUND OF THE **PEOPLE YOU ARE MEETING TO NEGOTIATE WITH.**

If you don't know the answer to these questions, **who** can you ask or **where** can you go to find more information about cultural differences?

# **18** Evaluating your performance

Answer the questions in this checklist after you have finished a negotiation. Your answers will help you to think about what you can do to improve your skills for the next time you are in a negotiation.

---

EVALUATION CHECKLIST

---

**The result**

|  | Yes | No |
|---|---|---|
| 1. Did we reach an agreement?<br>(If your answer to Question 1 is 'Yes', answer Questions 2 to 5.) | ☐ | ☐ |
| 2. Is the agreement better than the best alternative to negotiated agreement (BATNA)?<br>(The answer to this question should be 'Yes'.) | ☐ | ☐ |
| 3. Has the agreement been confirmed in writing? | ☐ | ☐ |

## EVALUATION CHECKLIST

**The result** (continued)                                    Yes    No

    4.   Is there any possibility of a misunderstanding about what we have agreed? ☐ ☐

    5.   Am I confident that the agreement will be long-lasting? ☐ ☐

---

**My negotiating skills: preparation**

    6.   Did I prepare for the negotiation as well as I should have done? ☐ ☐

    7.   Was I in difficulty at any time during the negotiation because I did not prepare fully? ☐ ☐

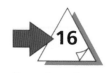

See also the preparation checklist in Chapter 16, *Preparing for a negotiation*.

## EVALUATION CHECKLIST

**Establishing rapport**                                                  Yes    No

8.  Did I establish **good rapport** with the other party?    ☐    ☐

---

**Starting the negotiation: discussion**

9.  Did we discuss the **purpose** of the meeting before    ☐    ☐
    we began to negotiate?

10. Did we set an **agenda** for the meeting?    ☐    ☐

    (If the answer to the Question 9 is 'No', would it    ☐    ☐
    have been a good idea to set an agenda?)

11. Did I explain my **interests and objectives** clearly?    ☐    ☐

12. Did I understand the interests and objectives of    ☐    ☐
    the other party?

13. Did I **listen actively** to what the other party was    ☐    ☐
    saying?

14. Did I check my understanding of their interests?    ☐    ☐

## EVALUATION CHECKLIST

**Starting the negotiation: discussion** (continued)    Yes    No

15. Did I use a variety of techniques to answer their questions?    ☐    ☐

16. Did I **listen** to and **observe** their reactions carefully?    ☐    ☐

**Proposing and bargaining**

17. Did I make **constructive proposals**?    ☐    ☐

18. Did I **remain positive** in my attitude?    ☐    ☐

19. When I did not agree with their proposals, did I **explain my reasons** clearly?    ☐    ☐

20. When I did not agree with their proposals, did I **make alternative suggestions**?    ☐    ☐

21. Did I use **signalling language** (to offer concessions)?    ☐    ☐

## EVALUATION CHECKLIST

**Proposing and bargaining** (continued)　　　　　　Yes　No

22. Did I **react to signals** from the other party?　☐　☐

23. Did I **link offers to conditions**?　☐　☐

24. Did I **trade** rather than give concessions?　☐　☐

25. Was I a **principled negotiator**?　☐　☐

**Handling problems**

26. Were there any problems in the negotiation?　☐　☐

27. How could they have been avoided?　☐　☐

28. Did I handle the problems well?　☐　☐

29. Did the problems prevent us from reaching a good agreement?　☐　☐

# EVALUATION CHECKLIST

**Reaching settlement**                                    Yes     No

    30.  Did we find **common ground**?

    31.  Did I check and clarify the agreement?

    32.  Did the negotiation end in a positive way which
        will contribute to future negotiations?

**General**

    33.  Did the other party surprise me with his or her
        approach to the negotiation?

    34.  Were cultural differences a problem during the
        negotiation?

# EVALUATION CHECKLIST

It is also useful to ask yourself the following questions:

What went well?

What went badly?

What language problems did I encounter?

What would I do differently next time?

| | Yes | I could do better next time | No |
|---|---|---|---|
| Am I satisfied with my performance in the negotiation? | ☐ | ☐ | ☐ |